Nothing

WAS A WASTE

ASHLEIGH RAYL

Nothing
WAS A WASTE

NOTHING WAS A WASTE
Written and Arranged by: Ashleigh Rayl

Edited by: Christina Strigas
Interior Design by: Maureen Cutajar
Cover Art by: Mitch Green

May you have faith in me always
to help guide you through this life.

DEDICATION

This book is dedicated to anyone
that has ever been there for me,
those who have ever loved and cared for me.
Who have never stopped fighting for me.
This is for those of you that have
given me hope and guidance.
This is for you Mom and Dad.
Without you I would not be who I am today.

This book is dedicated to my children.
To the precious two that were created inside of me
inches away from my heart.
You that have been and will always remain
the only people to ever get so close to it.
You are the air I breathe.
You are the sun that shines upon me everyday.
You are the greatest blessings that
I will ever receive in my life.
My reasons for being the best person I can be.
Cherish these words and pass this book down to your
children, and their children after that.
Keep me alive my loves for as long as you can,
so that even when I am long gone from this world,
this part of me will remain.
This piece of my soul, my precious words.
So that I may exist within the hearts and minds of my blood,
my beloved family, that I will never meet.

DEDICATION

This book is dedicated to anyone else that
needs these words.
I hope they reach you and help you.
Know that you are never alone with
where your feelings take you.
I am there.
I have faith that by reading this book you will see
that nothing in this life is a waste,
that there is beauty within everything.
Especially the pain.

TABLE OF CONTENTS

INTRODUCTION

These are the inside secrets
My minds endless stories
Of a spoiled little girl
A curious self sabotaging teen
A drug abuser
A real person that had to learn
how to love herself
A brave survivor
A fountain of undying possibilities
A triumphant recovered addict
A happy loving mother
A dedicated loyal warrior
Of a woman born again and again
Perceive them as you perceive them
Soak them in as your mind lets you see
These are my untold truths
Guiding you like subtitles on a screen
This is my significant honesty
Enjoy as you read where
life has brought me

The Mess

Have you ever made a mistake?

I'm sure you have.
We all do and so did I.

Mine was very monumental,
very life altering.
Forcing me to abandon myself
while another entity took my place.
As a child, I had no idea the
gravity of such a thing.
A mistake so compacted with temptation
that I fell victim to its deadly grip.
Picking up that alluring instrument,
filled with toxic pleasure,
was without a doubt a mistake
that would mark me for life.
It would become
an everlasting part of me.

Which is why it is so difficult
to even know where to begin
forgiving myself.

Understanding is what
fuels acceptance.
It aids us
to that clarity.
It seems that tragedies
never make sense.
That is what
makes them
so horridly unacceptable.

You watched me scream
until I couldn't breathe,
Shattering
Aching so badly
I couldn't sleep.
Shaken from the
bruises and bleeding.
Falling onto my knees,
Collapsing
Begging you to help me,
Breaking
But you never helped me.
You just laid there with me,
Breaking

Frustration overwhelms me,
brings me back
to my childish ways.
Back to that spoiled little girl,
back to my adolescent days.
It's like fire all around me,
I can't breathe from
all the flames.
The smoke fills my lungs
with uncontrollable rage.
Taking target
on my heart,
precision in its aim.
So intense it's like a dream.
I have to get it out.
I have to release it.
I have to scream.

What if I told you there's a hole in me?

That has never been covered.
Never been outside,
never seen by any eyes,
nor healed over.
What if I told you I destroy?
Hopes. Dreams. Goals. Visions.
Pull them down and bury them
behind a wall of comfortable stability.
What if I told you I burn houses?
Setting fire to the
sympathetic soul beneath,
collecting the tempered ashes.
What if I told you I hurt people?
Broken. Shattered. Changed forever.

What if you really knew what I've done?
Would you still trust me
with your heart?

Would you still love me?

She was always
difficult to love.
You had to adapt
completely around her.
She was like the weather.
You never knew
what to expect,
but you were
ready for whatever.
She was worth fighting for.
She was the golden needle
in the haystack.
You never could quite
figure out what
she wanted you to say,
or how she wanted you to act.
But you were willing to stay
at the end of the day,
and you changed yourself
to love her.

Unfortunately she craved
too much sweetness in life.
Always eating her
dessert for breakfast.
Never doing what was expected.
That for her was the
sweetest of all.
The inexplicable taste of deviation.

I look at myself
and I see another me,
with a shattered woman's
fingers in my hair,
and tall high heels on my feet.
The music starts playing.
They ask me if I am ready.
Here we go again my sweet
All eyes on me
I wonder if they can feel my pain,
If they can see my scars,
If they can sense my defeat?
Is that why they are so intrigued?
A hypnotizing performance,
rehearsed endlessly.
My hips project my
captivating agony.
My eyes are clouded over
for protection like a great white
on a feeding frenzy.
I'm someone else.
Still they are enticed.
They want more.
They want to know me,
little do they know I have
completely left my body.
I'm not here,
this is but a shell of me.

I don't share
my thoughts
with you
to prove
that I am right,
or to try and
change your mind.
I share
my thoughts
with you
mainly,
not to feel
so alone inside.

It has happened
ever since I was a little child.
I don't know how it was
instilled within me so deeply.
I dreamed of being seen by all,
always wanting
everyone to like me.
I yearned for acknowledgement.
Trying to impress everyone
and do whatever it was
I thought you would want to see.
I danced wildly in attention.
I wanted everyone to
fall in love with me,
so that they could
show me how to
fall in love with myself.

How is it that
just one heart
can love
so many
so deeply,
but yours can't
even love one.

I've cried so much
I can't keep track

I'm not sure if I've already died.

Sitting here on this couch again
evaporating inside.

This death I invite.
I show it the way,
straight to my heart,
several countless times a day.
Practically begging for
it's dangerous comfort
every single time.

What am I doing?
What do I honestly expect?

I can't stand to think anymore,
laying in a bed of painful regrets.

Why does it hurt so much
living this empty life of mine?
Why do I chose this?
Why can't I leave it behind?

They ask me
Why do you live in these places?

They ask me why
Why do I take risks so carelessly?

I have another question for them
Who should I be
afraid of in this world,
when no one can hurt me
like me?

He chose to love me
at my bottom.
When the desperation
in me raged.
He was always there
helping me
pick up the pieces
of the never ending
destruction
I was causing.
Through it all
he had the nerve
to tell me
that I was
still the one.

The one he found
most beautiful.

Have you ever seen water
cut patiently *but*
viciously *through rock?*

Forming anew to its
forceful persistency.
Molding rocks that
are durable as ever
with its crumbling power.
For it is not always
an intimidating appearance.
The patience,
the dedication,
the extraordinary power
it holds within its waves
is what really frightens me
about water.

All I've
ever wanted
was to look
in the mirror
and see
that beautiful
girl everyone
tells me about.

These breaths are suffocating.
The air Is too thick for me.
The sight is overbearing.
I can't seem to see
what needs to be seen.
All I hear is screaming.
I'm going deaf with disbelief.
With so much chaos
around me, no one sees
what's underneath.
That place you speak of
Serenity
Turns into an illusion before
my very eyes.
I just can't seem to get there.
It's a tragic shame
that this is how I'll die.

I didn't see a light,
I didn't hear him
speak to me.
It was blackness,
it was darkness
for the moments
I was completely empty.
It was not life changing,
It was not scary,
at least not to me.
The only feeling
I felt was remorse,
for the ones
that almost lost me.

You say that
sometimes
I am naive.
That what I
worry about
is ridiculous,
that I have
a childish mind.
Your so much
older I guess
that must be so.
But I cannot see
that if the
naive one
is me.

How is there
so much that
you don't understand?

You were like dry leaves
Engulfed by my flame
So blindly in love
So fragile
So unprepared
You never stood a chance
Nonetheless
I am completely to blame
You see my pet
There is no future as us
For me
There is pleasure
For you
There will only be pain

-message from the pen

I've never loved more deeply,
for that of a dying creature.

*Why is it that we can
openly and properly
appreciate one another
when death is forefront?*

If you think about it

*Are we all not dying as well,
perhaps just a bit more gradually?*

I was blindly
stepping forward.
Out amongst
the miscreants
of the world.
Ready to join them,
ready to rule
the lowlives.
I was lost between
a woman and a child.
Impressionable
I had quite an appetite
for destruction.
I'm not sure if I'll ever
get that bitter taste
out of my mouth.

Some women are givers
Relentlessly fighting for others
Some women are providers
Inexhaustibly establishing a home
Some women are monsters
Some women are saviors
But her
She was a taker
Always wanting more
Wanting it all
She would overthrow the throne
She would do it
A thousand times over
Even if that meant she'd end up
All alone

I've never hated myself
more in these moments.
These moments when
I think of you.

Another dose of oblivion please

I was always insane,
always doing
the same things,
expecting
my heart
not to break.
Hoping
the results
would change.
Praying that
I'd have the
strength
to just
stop
one day.

I can't breathe
I'm suffocating
In this dreadfully tight space
I can't see
through the shameful putrid fog
I can't hear you
I'm buried too deeply
My body stands hollow
I am empty
I sacrificed myself
For false deliverance
All that remains
Is the demon
That I followed here

She walked home every night.
No fear in her heart,
no worries in her mind,
no planted monstrosities
of any kind.

That innocent little girl
was about to learn
a hard merciless lesson
from the world
she would never leave behind.

As I sit here
in my favorite black dress
with tear soaked eyes
and an aching heart,
I can't help but think
how much of a
beautiful honor it is
to hurt this much.

To miss you this much.

To have had the life
changing opportunity
of loving you.

Don't be ashamed of me
I'm only you
Don't be embarrassed
I'll go away soon
Don't be frustrated
I'll be back again
In a different way,
on a different stage.

Our binding fate
Will never end.

I don't understand
how I can love myself
when all I see
are the mistakes
I have made,
these precious people
I have hurt,
and this guilt
I hold so closely.
I am utterly
disgusted with me.

Am I completely lost?
Will I ever be free?

I was born so
uniquely beautiful.
So magically and
purely myself,
but unfortunately
somehow,
throughout my life
I have convinced myself
that I want
to be somebody else.

Losing her was like
Throwing
The rarest of diamonds
Into the sea
I'll never come
Across another like her
I had no idea
How special she was
Or how empty
Life without her
Could be

You've lived so long
Down there
You've found comfort
In the flames
Trapped
By perception
Engulfed
By feeble thoughts
Blinded
By weakness
It's never made you happy
But you've adapted
To the fire
You can handle
This hell

How is it that one becomes
so tempted by the darkness?

Before you blink twice
you can fall into its seduction.
It's just so
alluring and peculiar,
the ease of it.

Are we all meant to fall
at the very beginning?

Yes she was beautiful,
yes she was unique.
A heart and personality
that made you
want to belong in her world.
A marvelous
one of a kind inspiration
whose intelligence
edged greatness.
She was just so interesting.
She had it all,
as so it seemed.
But in the end
it was the insecurities
and doubts she held
deep inside her,
right at the edge
that nobody else seen,
that took her from us.
Her weaknesses had prevailed.

What a mask she wore.

What monsters she hid.

She was my best friend.
Our major was destruction.
Dancing all day and night
in her river of fire.
She gave me companionship
that I searched for in
countless others.
She gave me a perception
of the world outside my
confused own.
She was my crutch to a
broken heart.
A way for me to
drown in myself
without having to hear
the screams inside.
Shutting the doors of the
rooms in my mind that
haunted me.
I let her have
too much control though.
I could barely
get off my knees.
Burnt to a crisp.
She left me wondering alone
like an abandoned child.
I used her and she used me.

Can't see beyond this obsession
Lost in the abstracted fog
The instantaneous satisfaction

Always wins

Leaving me with just
Little fragmented memories
Of what I've done

We have matching
luggage once again.
Those bags under your eyes,
they look strikingly familiar.
We both have had sleepless nights.
Whatever the reason may be,
we will get through it.
We can't stay awake forever.
That's the thing
about being human.
We have to fall asleep eventually.

How can I tell you
I think you can do anything?
That I think you're amazing,
that I think you're beautiful.
How can I tell you
that we can make it?
That I love you,
that we can do better.
How can I tell you
that I think you're worth it?
That you matter.
How can I tell you
how crazy it makes me
when you can't see that?
You are so special to me,
we are all we have.
You *are* important.
Yet all you see
is negativity and pain.
It truly is the hardest
and an undoubtedly
tragic thing
to still believe in yourself,
but be trapped inside
someone who made up
there mind long ago
that they are *unworthy.*

That was the
thing about her,
she never broke down
in front of anyone.
So afraid to be seen
as such a fragile little thing.
So put together
until she was alone.

We are all our own monsters.
Those thoughts you think about,
the ones you have to
hurry and stop
your mind from thinking about.
I imagine you
surprise yourself with
such thoughts.
You could burn in those thoughts.
You cannot run or hide
from the darkness
that lies within us all.
You must have control.
There are some places
we must never go
even if that place
is in ourselves.

I should have known better,
but I made a mistake.
I trusted the wrong person.
I had faith in a selfish man.
He should have known
I couldn't handle the needle.
He knew I would get lost
in this death dealing game,
but he couldn't go in by himself.
So I regretfully did,
we both did.
Didn't know where to go
or which way was out.
Luckily I found salvation
on my own.
It's a shame
I couldn't of helped him,
but he could not escape himself.
I escaped.
I set myself free.
Once I got out
it was really very easy,
to never go back
to such a man again.

I cannot do this anymore.
I don't care about the money.
I see an angel trapped
behind your eyes,
and when I look at you
she speaks to me.
Leave here and never return.
I cannot be apart of this.
I cannot watch such misery.
I love you precious
with all my heart.
Is what she said to me.

-message from my drug dealer

As I climbed
the stairs of salvation,
I humbly thank God
for opening the gate.
I have prayed
to him every night
on my knees,
after each and every break.
Finally he
has acknowledged
my cries.
Knowing that
that was all I could take.

My heart and stomach are ice cold.
I cannot feel my fingers or toes.
My body is on fire.
My insides scream bloody murder.
I am sweaty,
I am freezing,
I cannot stop shaking.
Such a gruesome transformation,
ripping this demon out of me.
I have never felt such pain before.

Everything ends eventually
Stay strong
and hold on,
we are almost free.

It was the smell,
not so much the pain,
that I will never
be able to forget.
The rancid stench
of a sinful girl
dying and decaying
on the floor.
Helplessly fighting
through the
demented withdrawals.
That stink of agonizing
metamorphosis.
It will forever haunt me.
I've never gushed
such a scent
since that day.

The Clean Up

The shower has always
been my haven.
It is my happy place.
The tender steam,
the warm state.
I always found peace
in the shower.
The water pouring
over me,
washing all the
pain away,
and in that moment
everything is serene.
The voices stop,
my fear is gone,
and my heart feels free.
It is a very calm
and tranquil place for me.

You'll never forget it.
There is no way you can.
Those tainted memories
will forever live inside.
It's a scary thing
to realize and stare in the face.
Seeing what you're capable of,
but it's a beautiful thing
to see what you will not allow.
That pain and fear.
That sickness and despair.
That coldness you feel
in your stomach.
Truly bad people,
sociopaths,
do not feel that.
There is no remorse for the evil.
You have to remember
no matter what you've done
it's done
all that matters now
is what you'll do.

Remember my dear,
that it is over,
you pulled yourself through.

In just ten seconds
my thoughts ran rapid,
and my heart was unsettled.
Anxiety seeped out of my pours
from the nauseating humidity,
but I chose right over wrong
Instinctively
There was no other choice for me.
I never thought
those demons I faced
would bring to life my
hope and faith
in something great.

She always
Yearned
For something more
Much more
Than anyone
Could give
She searched
For it in
Many things
Other days
She merely hid
It's not like
She wanted
The world
Just someone
To understand her
And forgive her
For what she did

Beneath the skin
I fall from
unquestionable defeat,
but slowly rise to my feet.
For I know another battle
is soon to be won.
As the shadows escape
around the illuminated sun.
Yielded by my crippled intellect,
and all the dots
I still cannot connect.
My heart grows fiercely firm,
as I sit ready for the
next lesson
I must learn.

You cannot fool me
I know the horrors in your soul.
The transgressions you
have committed.
The demon within you,
behind the person you
try to hide behind.
A translucent ghost
put forth by a fabricated lie.
A girl unweathered,
very pretty on the outside,
but I've seen your monster.
I've watched you destroy people
with empty dry eyes.
I wonder how long it will be
until she returns.
Until your old
selfish self is revived.

–message from the doubters

It is though
I have two people
living beneath my
fragile skin.
One who is
logical and rational,
holding all the
answers before I
even begin.
One who is
weak and destructive,
causing
disorganized chaos,
never allowing
me to win.

I will never go back to that girl.
No one can ever make me.
I have control over myself now.
I will not go out without a fight.
Although the victory is
sometimes not so easy.
I have found faith within my hands
they will never again disobey me.

They could barely
keep up with me,
my mind has continuous
anxious crazy thoughts.
All competing and fighting
to get my attention.
Talking about this,
curious about that.
Thinking and thinking.
It is constant.
They always pondered
what I would chose
to let escape.
They wondered
what I would do.

Removing yourself
from an atmosphere
or from a person
that makes you feel
like a bad person
is not a weak move.
In fact it is a
courageous one,
of the utmost
intelligent kind.
To protect
yourself always,
not just your heart,
but also your mind.

Allow me to apologize
for everything
that I let happen.
Look at the bright side
you'll never go through
this all alone.
I'll be here for you

Always

Until our last breath.
For we are one
Forever together
until our death.

-message from self

Be who you are.
Do not be ashamed of
your wild beauty.
For even a tornado
As uncontrollable
And destructive
as it is,
is quite breathtaking
when it is it's
true powerful self.

I had no idea that love
could be so infinite.
After tearing your heart apart
with my frail ruthless hands,
showing no mercy.

Lost

Still you fought for me,
even when there wasn't
much left to fight for.

−I'm sorry Mom

When I least expect it the
should haves devour me.

Starting from my toes
Eating it's way up my legs,
biting up and down my shoulders
until it sets it's teeth
into my neck.
There it whispers it's
sweet regret.

You should have done this
You should have done that
You should have
You should have

Regret flows into defeat,
defeat flows into disappointment.
Disappointment flows
into sadness,
and by the time
I realize what has happened
I've become so
strangely used to it,
that I don't even cry.

What a world
It would be
If we buried
Not just bodies
But buried
Love
As well
When it died
The earth
Would be
Overwhelmed
With graves
The streets
Would run
Red with
Heartache
Everywhere
We would go
We would be
Walking on
Heartbreak

People will
frequently come
into your life
and will leave behind
impressions like
footprints in dirt.
The kind that
wash away with the rain,
that are forgotten
after a short time.
Special are the few
that come in and
leave imprints on our souls.
Like footprints in cement,
leaving behind a mark
of themselves forever.
Even if they should leave.

I spent my day searching
for apologies once again.
They say it's not enough
to simply speak the words,
but I feel that's the only way
to make this regret end.
For my "sorry"s are not
just hollow gifts,
they hold inside my
awareness and remorse,
on a slender shaky fingertip.

I've held my
tongue in frustration
Most of the
time in fear.
For I never
know what
words
will come
out of me,
it is always
my cross to bear.

She was a magician,
putting on a spectacular show.
Performing the most
alluring acts.
It made her inaccessible though,
because deep down inside
she thought love also
was just an illusion.
It would take
considerably more than
the quick slide of hand
to trick her heart
into believing
it was real.

I sleep with monsters
living inside my head.
I lay staring blankly
as they scream
so loudly.
They speak of pain,
they speak of doubt.
I have to actively
stop them and
completely shut
them out.
They speak of the past,
of the days
that I once knew
They speak of
heartache,
and they speak of you.

Another year passes
and yet still we are apart.
I don't understand it
Inside it leaves me helpless.
I just don't know what to do.

Do you think of me?
Did you ever love me?
Do you even actually care?

I'll always have this void,
and unfortunately
you'll always
be morbidly special to me,
because you were
the first person
in my life
to tell me that I
was not good enough
for you.

And if you could leave,
Who else will leave too?

If she saw hearts
instead of faces.
If she could see
the precious inside
past the mask,
the true being,
the spirit that
inhabits within.

I wonder if she
would be any
different,
and how
different
would she be?

When you fell in
love with me,
you fell only
for my flowers.
Neglecting the
true beauty
of my roots.
So when
winter approached,
and my petals
withered away.
You left.
Not even realizing
I would ever as before
bloom again.

My expectations of myself
have almost become
pure fantasy.
It's time to embrace
what is real.
I yell often,
I over think things a lot,
I lie sometimes,
I make a fool out of myself,
but I try my best each day.
I know and I realize
these things,
and I'm working on it.
Nothing great was built
in a moment,
in a minute,
in a single solitary way.
I know I need to
have patience with myself,
and calm down.
I'll get there some day.

Right now
There isn't much to do
She can either
Build herself up
Or destroy herself
No one on this earth
Can do it better than her
All we can do is
Be here with her
While she decides
What she is going to do

I am far more attracted
to how you see yourself,
how you see the world,
how you see others.
The way you look
is of little
significance to me.
The fact that you
bear exceptional beauty,
is of course all you
could possibly be.

Some days in the mirror,
when I catch a glimpse
of myself I end up staring
right into my eyes
wondering how much
of me is truly me,
and how much am I
of so many others
transfigured into this
girl staring at me.

I may not see
it today or tomorrow,
but one day
I'll be able to look back
and be completely perplexed
at how everything worked out.
Those torturous nights
when I thought
I wouldn't make it.
Where I thought I'd
lost myself entirely.
I didn't
I'm grateful that I
never gave up.
So many others do.
I made it through
All those long days
brought me to right here,
this life.
I have to cherish it
Embrace the reality
and love myself.
Forgive myself,
because I made it.
Now it's time for me to rebuild.

Are we all not good and bad?

Angel and demon
co-existing within flesh
within one soul,
a single mind.
It is precisely how we
balance the two
that makes us our true selves.

Who we really are inside.

Cease yourself
from walking in fear.
Constantly looking
behind you.
Pain is not a residual ghost.
It will not follow you,
it will not haunt you,
unless you invite it to.
So stop

My actions are
permanent and forceful.
There is no taking them back,
there is no undoing them.
What's done is done
as they say.
I'm still
understanding
the consequences,
the depth and
damage of some.
That my actions
are a statement and
a representation
of who I am
and what I become.

Do not be afraid to love
because of the hurting.
The aftertaste of heartbreak
is how you remember
the delicious first kiss.

I reminded myself of an
incomprehensible book.
Complicated storyline,
perplexing chapters,
extraordinary characters.
I was an
everlasting curiosity
to myself.
Just when I thought I had it
all figured out,
the plot would change.
I never could quite
figure me out.
Though I always tried,
I tried so hard.

As you grow older
you will see
that we all do
things that cause
us shame.
It's unavoidable
in this life.
You must look
inside your heart
and focus only on
what kind of
knowledge it brings,
and not get lost
in the pain.

Can you remember it?

The first time you
tasted sin.
The first time you
intentionally
broke a rule.
Disobeyed
Deciding not to listen
to what you were told to do.

Or has it been too long?

So long
that you don't even
remember
what its like to
have known
innocence.

I always identified
with her to not feel
so alone, but
I don't want to be Alice.

Lost in her
disputable wonderland.
Fearfully indecisive
about herself.
Adrift in the prodigious sea
of her own.
Unsure of all her
unique capabilities.
No, I don't want to be Alice

At long last
I want to be me.
But who is that really?

I always hope
you'll be there.
That I'll get
to see you.
To touch and kiss you,
to have you play a part
in my mysterious world
they call a dream.
For in my dreams
my reality has no control,
and I'm running solely
on my hearts desires.

I could do it no more,
I was tired,
I was ashamed.
I couldn't represent it
any longer.
I had to let it go.
It was like a
violent tsunami
of emotions,
waves ripping
right through me,
swallowing me whole.
I did it
I made it out alive.
Never again will I
allow myself to be
so vulnerable.

She was not at all the person
she once was in her past,
she has changed a lot,
give her a chance.
She is different.
You should not
think of her
as just the same troubled girl
that she was before.
She is better.
That part of her
has transformed into
something new.
She has been altogether
altered and the rest
was shunned,
but still remains
the memory of
who she was
and what she has done.

You can escape
anything.
The past
hasn't changed,
but I have.
The memories remain,
but my soul
has been forgiven.
I made it through
all of the shame.
So grateful for
the new life
I have been given.
A fresh new start
away from
all the pain.

In the times of despair
Those times you
can't even breathe
When your stomach
is ice cold,
and your heart too.
She was something
unbelievable.
The composure she emanated,
and the pain she hid
was in itself
a beautifully conducted
and controlled rise of
who she wanted to be.
Through epic
destruction
and unexpected betrayal,
arose an
imperfect creation
of her true self
she has been waiting
her whole life to see
unveiled.
It was a sight to see
and it was magical.
She should be
ever so proud
of herself.

The Shine

She sits and watches
as the world goes by.
Grabbing at every little
piece of happiness
that she can get her
hands on.
She see's those eyes,
she falls in love with
that smile.
Patiently she sets her aim
on him.

In that moment,
she changed.

Just like that.
In those minutes
she evolved into
a different version
of herself,
with a new purpose.

A reason for being better.

That lost little
girl that was
once so lonely.

Who searched
tirelessly for love
and acceptance.

She found it
at last
In his arms.

I understood my worth
which made me powerful.
That innocent child needed
A warrior
A leader
so I became one,
a magnificent one.

He looked up to me,
he adored me.

Through the patient
loving guidance
I administered,
I made him into
a warrior as well
and he loved me for it.

When we create another life,
we are making it anew.
Everything we do,
every word we speak,
every action we perform
is a cementation of their being.
Everything you are
will transfuse into their soul.
Your weaknesses and strengths,
your fears and doubts,
your beauty and hope.
For whatever children absorb,
we are responsible.
So set an impeccable example.
Teach them tactics you
didn't learn until belated in life.
Imprint your optimal qualities.
Hope they soak up
your sunshine,
and prepare them
for the rain.

He changed
my life that day.

He rearranged
my priorities.

He fixed my
soul in an instant.

A moment is all it took.

With a simple smile,
with those little eyes,
with a single
unforgettable look.

A brand new world,
a blank white slate.
Let me open your eyes.
So many magnificent
things to see.
The stars in the sky,
the songs in the wind,
the beauty in the trees.

It's a brand new world
my precious baby

For you and for us.

It would seem as though
I *completely* overcame
my darkness.
Withholding my selfish
intentions and beliefs.
Surviving myself entirely.
Coming out of it
a much better me,
and yes it is so
a rightful voice
I have achieved.
But still I fight
her everyday,
it is a constant
war underneath.

I choose to be me.
I will not change for
anything or anybody.
Sure I could adjust some things,
evolve gradually,
adapt to my surroundings.
I'll still be who I am,
I'll still be me.
As my daughter grows up
this she will see.
It's the greatest gift I could give.
The best example I could seek.
Hopefully,
if I do it all successfully,
she will love herself entirely
for whom she is.
All because I chose to be me.

Dear my sweet child,

The fight within you will be the hardest
longest, most tiring fight
you'll ever go through
But keep fighting
Cage that part of you
that pulls you down
That part that tells you, you can't do it
you won't make it, you can't handle it
That part that rushes forward to react
before you get a chance to have a
single rational thought
That part that constantly judges you
That part that leaves you with
nothing but
embarrassment and disappointment
That part you cry your eyes out over
You feel like you have no control over it, but you do sweetie
This is but a piece of you
Find a safe place for it
Don't let the weakness consume you
You are stronger.
You have so much power.
You are more than just that piece
Never stop fighting for that balance
Fight for it hard
Regain your control
Because you are so much more

Love, your mother

I'm just a simple girl I think.
I smile when I'm told
I'm beautiful,
though at many times
I don't seem to see it.
I have so many blessings
in my life,
though I always stress unnecessarily.
I'm almost always being
silly or joking,
though at times it is a mask,
when inside I'm drowning.
Sometimes I work
really hard at things.
Sometimes I fail and
sometimes I win
I am who I am,
and I love me
Maybe I am not so simple,
though I am simply me.

There I found
My purpose

I found
My patience

I found
My divine importance

I found
My happiness

It is all so true

I found it all
In those little eyes

I found it all
In you

Her eyes were glistening,
and were as black as
the night.
If you looked closely
you could see yourself
completely
inside of them.
A reflection of your true self.
Those that got a glimpse
crumbled to their knees.

They are
fierce and powerful
on their own,
but together they are an unstoppable team.
They lean on each other
for not just
everlasting support
and security,
but for the growth
and happiness
their lives bring
one another.

As I sit here gazing into those eyes
my heart skips a beat,
and my soul sinks into my body.
Overwhelmed with happiness
it crashes over me like
an euphoric wave.
My cheeks ache from the smile.
It's almost like a drug.
The way their laughter rushes through my veins.
Sparking a feeling wondrously incomparable
to any I've ever felt before.
Being a mother is the most
powerful satisfaction
I could have ever imagined.
Those two magical pieces of me
formed into new unique beings
are mine forever,
and I'm addicted for life.

I think too much
I think way too much
I think ahead
I think behind
I think sideways
I think sharp
I think blind

There is so much
constantly at work up there.
Far too much for a tender mind.
I could think myself
into a coma like sleep,
where all those thoughts
could transfer into dreams,
and each little one
could be set free.

She was the
kind of shock
that would take you
off of your feet.
That took your
breath away.
That made your heart
skip a beat.

I owe not an explanation
for my flaws.
I owe not a justification
for my mistakes.
I owe not a clarification
for my choices.
I am what I am.
I have my moments.
Not always the
sharpest knife,
but I'm growing
and I'm learning.
Let me live my damn life.

My looks are but one of the
Many reasons why you'll
Never find another like me
My loyalty
My hope
My weirdness
My understanding
My mind
My heartbreak
My honesty
My compassion
My love
Knowing just the way
To make you smile
I promise you won't
Find all that's in me
In anyone else
You seek

Nothing holds you back
more than your
own insecurities.
I promise you
the world doesn't
even notice
the things you worry
so much about.

Stop living under
that illusionary
microscope

Let yourself live,
effortlessly.

Child you know nothing
of enduring pain.
Of really bearing
the worst of the worst.
You can't imagine
what people can go through
and manage to stay alive.
The barbarity the
body can take.
How us as glorious
humans will always survive.

I never knew what job I wanted
to do when I grew up,
I just knew what sort of person
I wanted to be.
I wanted to be proud of myself,
to stand strong on my own.
I wanted to provide
my own money.
I wanted to be
structured and stable,
but most of all
I didn't want to rely
on anyone else emotionally.
Money has never been
a problem for me,
it's understandable and stationary.
My emotions on the other hand
have always been
very confusing
especially to me.

My heart cannot help
but to take on the
emotions of poetry.
Carrying others pain
on my shoulders.
Weeping another's tears.
The sadness of their story
infiltrates my very soul.

Never doubt yourself my love.
Not what you are,
nor what you can do.
You can change the world
with the right state of mind
and a strong set of tools.

If you think about it
everything has always
worked out for you.

You worry
You stress

You over think every
possible and impossible
scenario and outcome.
Even though that is just you
and you can't help it sometimes,
practically all the time.
If you could just somehow
remind yourself to
trust in this life.
Try to calm your mind and believe
that everything will be just fine
because it will be alright.

Hasn't it always?

I want to know it all.
I want to know everything,
but what is so ironic
is that some of the things
I already know
and understand
utterly terrify me.

Feeling fear has always
kept me sane.
I couldn't imagine
the type of
devastation and destruction
I would be capable
of causing,
if I was not afraid.

I look at her
and she reminds me
of another little girl
I once knew.

I wonder when
I was a child if I once
looked at you
and was reminded of
yourself too, Mom.

I get angry
I get frustrated
I throw childlike fits
I express my thoughts
I speak my mind
My actions usually
Spawn from my emotions
I have many flaws
I will always make mistakes
But I stand up for myself
For what I feel
What I see
And what I truly believe
I will never apologize
Or be ashamed
Ever again
For being me

We live in a world that
thinks suffering is riveting.
Enchanted by the thought
that it will make you notable.
Universally spread
across the globe.
We welcome pain,
because most of us
honestly know
nothing of it.

She was one of the rare ones
that never had been seen.
She was a crisp fall morning
with an ice cold breeze.
The sun was always
shining though,
so you didn't want to leave.
So chillingly herself,
like nothing you could believe.

Who am I?

I'm made from all the
people I've encountered,
the things I've seen.
Beneath I hold all my thoughts
translated into feelings,
happiness from
unexpected situations,
irrational fears molded
by my imagination.
I'm stitched together
from the personalities
of my parents,
and the stepping stones
I've acquired throughout my life.
I am an imperfect creation
of many things
spun into one
exclusive self.

I stopped wishing that
one morning
I'll wake up
and be the woman
I've always wanted to be.
Transformed in every way.
It takes much longer
than I expected.
I had to be patient with myself.
Now I'm doing it.
I'm becoming her,
little by little,
day by day.

Never be ashamed
of your story.
Everything you've
been through
has brought you
To this moment
To this reality
To this world
You may have taken
some broken bones
and bruises along the way,
but it was worth it
because you survived
and just look
at what you've won.

I form every single one
Of my written words
Into translucent glass
So the lucky can see
Me inside them

Call me naïve
Call me gullible
But you can never
Call me close-minded
I believe in speaking
To people with your soul
Being vulnerable
Being raw
And doing what you can
To understand
I try to understand
Everything
To relate
To see things
Through the eyes of others
But hold on tightly
To my own perception

I'm just a woman
who chooses to live
in positivity.
No more pain
or judgments for me.
I see the light
many others just
can't see.
For all my
understanding
has brought me
to become,
the very best
person I can be.

Their childish laughter
dances around me
like joyous autumn leaves.
Their curiosity of life
frightens me,
blows through me
like a frosty powerful breeze.
Their selfless love
it calms me,
it sets me heart at ease.
Their smiles sink into me
like the cozy warmth
of the sun.
They make me appreciate
things I never did before.
I can't wait to see
what other wondrous emotions
they bring to my life.
I'm ready for more

Her compelling desire
to forgive people
slowly faded as
she realized not
everyone can change.

You are so
Hard on yourself
All the time
The judgments
The accusations
The shame
You don't even realize
How so many others
Would be lost
Without you
They would never be
The same

You always wanted
him to open up.
You wanted to understand him.
You wanted to cherish
and love him.
Living each day together.
Conversating about life
as you grew older.
You longed for
the interaction.
The soul bearing talks
You try not to upset him,
aiming to please,
because their was
nothing as irritating
as his silence.
Nothing as cold
as his cold shoulder.
He always knew how
to drive me crazy.
Always knew it was
shutting me out.

My thoughts
are so abundant.
They infiltrate my
every dream.
We kiss and touch,
we embrace each other.
It was only when
I awoke to find myself
all alone,
that I realized
it was not real.
We're not together
anymore.

You cannot stay sad sweetheart.
That is where you lose it
and the negativity spirals.
A vortex of endless dying hope.
You cannot go on thinking that
someone, somewhere
will give you all the answers.
It is only you that can
calm these thoughts
before the flood rushes through.
Yet everything
has always worked out.
You've always picked
up the pieces.
Rebuilt and moved on
As long as you stay
strong in your world
things will always work out.

You worry too much

But my god dear, you can be an unbelievable hurricane.
Looking in your eyes
I can't help but understand
why they name
such storms after people.

Every once in a while you see
That sparkle
You feel that strength
And you understand
That everything
You've ever gone through
In your life
Has brought you to here
And I don't know about you
But there's no where else
I'd rather be

A smile
This small gesture
Can do wonders
It can rejuvenate
The broken
Validate the lost
Bring comfort
To the fractured
But nobody can
Smile for you
It must come
From within
You have to
Possess that
Happiness
To dole it out
So look deep
Inside yourself
And decide
Do you have
What it takes
To smile

He may be quiet and closed,
while I'm an open book.
He might be
simple and uncomplicated,
while I'm colorful and complex.
He may be everything I'm not,
my total opposite.
I'm grateful to experience
such unfamiliar things,
because we share a beautiful
reliable kind of love,
that makes perfect sense to me.

Darling you are
so dramatic

You know not a thing
of real terror.

Real fear
Real pain

But in all actuality
I don't either.
Yes I have suffered,
but it has all been
pretty much
Self inflicted
I could of stopped
at any time.

So for this weakness
who are we to blame?

Never better than,
but always thriving.
Always looking up.
No one is better
than anyone else.
I'm not sure how
that even came into
existence
Maybe we were
made this way?
The drive
The motivation
To be the best
To be better than
We all have the same
opportunity to think
more positively,
and change our lives
to better our own
unique situations.

Love yourself
Do not compare
Be a better you
Never better than

You stress too much my dear
People you don't even know
Think you are incredible
Forgive yourself
Give yourself a break
You are incredible

As the tide rolls in
all she could do was
stare off into the sunset.
Taking in the beauty
of her surroundings
and soaking up the relaxing
warmth against her face
from the setting sun.
Analyzing all the majestic
blessings that were bestowed
upon her.
In that moment
She became so peaceful
so content
so happy

Although she never thought
perfection was real,
she had to admit
she has come pretty damn close.

There is nothing
more admirable
than a person whom can see
the beauty beyond
the wreck.
A complete and freeing feeling
that must be.
To walk and live in positivity.
It's something
others yearn for,
and something many others
may never see.

I think I've always
had multiple personalities.
I think we all do in a way.
The runner and the fighter
The child and the adult
We pull out who
we need to when we must.
To protect ourselves,
with whatever and whoever,
has scientifically been
instilled into us.

I loved you with
such ease.
It was a
breathtakingly new
experience for me.
I just knew
I never ever
wanted to lose it.
I don't ever want
to meet the woman
I would be
without you
my darling.

My love
If I could teach you
one simple
yet powerful thing.
I would tell you
what feels better
than attention.

Confidence

Confidence feels
profoundly better.

Sometimes I wish
I could read your mind
That it'd be easier
For me to understand
But then other times
I wonder if I could handle all
The truth I would be reading

I get so blinded
With negativity
That sometimes
All I seem to see
Is the toys everywhere
Pizza again for dinner
The dishes
The laundry
The times I got so frustrated
And yelled
All they see is
My strength
My eternal love
They see their hero
Trying her best
They see their Mom
They will always see
The best in me
So relax
Just breathe

My sweet dear child,
don't you worry
about someone
not liking you.
They are probably
so desperately tormented
with trying to learn
how to like themselves.
You are a mirror to them,
or it could just be jealousy.

I'm here to
show you
the beauty
in this life,
and shield
you from
the horrors
I have lived.

If I did not contain fear,
if I did not
worry excessively,
if I did not overwater
my beautiful garden,
if I did not obsess
over the simple things.
Then I definitely
would not be me.
My flaws are what
completes me.

She obviously loved him.
She will always love him.
But even better
she desired him
day after day,
year after year,
above everyone else in this world.
She wanted only him,
and was committed to only him.
Beyond compromises
she didn't have to make.
Beyond all the changes.
She would have adjusted
the sun in the sky
for him.
Above it all stood
her loyalty,
her hopeful faith in his eyes.
She held a precious dedicated
kind of love for him.
More importantly she
believed in him
she desired him
day after day,
year after year.

Good things
happen to her because
she puts blessings out
into the world.

She lives them
She breathes them

She knows blessings never fail.
They come back loyally like a pet.
It may not be in that instant,
it may take a while,
but they are out there
waiting for her.
Things may happen in life,
but sadness fades.
It is never night forever.
The reliable sun always
shines again.
She's not going to do things
that break her joy.

Today is all she has
and she's going to make the
best of it.

If no one told you
it's never too late
to change.
If you don't like yourself
Change
Do something you
ordinarily would not do,
pick anything.
It's all in your control.
Own it
This is your world.
I hope you live a life
that you're proud of,
and if your not,
I hope you find
the strength to
start over
and create
something great.

She never seemed shattered to me
She was a breathtaking abstract
Painting of all the troubles
She had been through
That she overcame
And is still overcoming
She was inspiring
She was real
She was exactly who she was
Meant to be

Accept yourself as you are

That is the most difficult thing
in this world to some people.
It goes against their very instincts
Their education
Their culture
From the very beginning
we have been told and taught
to follow rules.
All of these rules.
Told how you should be.
Accepting yourself is the
glorious precious gem of this life,
because it goes against
the rules sometimes,
and against those judgments
you found out who you are
and you have come to love it.

It always fascinated me
that I could lucid dream.
The awareness fueled
something inside of me.
It was exceptional.
A place where normally
your subconscious rules
and you are stuck blinded
by the scenario you're thrown into.
I knew this game,
I knew the rules,
and how to follow them.
I can't quite explain the feeling,
but I do know how
to describe the ending.
That's the thing about realizing
you're in a dream.
You also know without
a doubt that's it is going to end.
Once that is released from
your mind,
it's only a matter of time
before your eyes open.

As you're sitting there
thinking about your life
and what you should do,

Try to remember these two things

No amount of guilt
can change what has happened
No amount of anxiety
can change what is
supposed to happen

The best way to approach things
is if you maintain positivity
and prepare yourself.
Stay strong
so that you may smile
through the struggles,
and be the rock
they need you to be.

I get so selfish at times
Surrounded by my feelings
So lost in all my own problems
Absorbed in my own world
That I forget
Without you
I wouldn't have one

Shush now dear

Allow yourself to just
breathe in this moment.

Shush now
Be quiet

Maybe this is where
you realize
you can stop
searching,
you already
have it all.

If you hear harsh things about me,
just look at who the person
it is coming from.
There might have been a time
that I was good to them.
I trusted them
Treated them with
love and respect.
Laughed with them
Cried with them
but they betrayed me.
They broke my heart,
so I had to leave them
Heartlessly

For that my friend
is a far different story.

This life of mine
I cannot see
Being any different
Any different at all
I love every minute of it
The great times
The struggles
The rewards
This is it
I am finally happy
I never thought
This could be

What screws us up the most in life
is the picture in our heads
of what and how it is
supposed to be.
We don't know how
it manifested this way,
but it did,
and there is no escaping it now.
It's like a disease,
once you have it
it is there for life.
You can learn to live with it
Cope
Deal with it
Balance your morals
and your outlook.
Make decisions
off what you think
you truly believe.
As long as you can find
that ability to separate
your illusionary picture
and just do what comes
blissfully naturally.
It won't matter what was
supposed to be,
because it's much more
precious just the way it is.

Let me show you
how to live
without constantly
being at war
with yourself.
Wars are not
always physical.
At least those
wars are simple.
It's kill or
be killed
Two enemies
fighting
one another,
but the emotional war
is the truly scary one,
because you are
fighting yourself.

The moon still shines
Always
Bringing a glimmer of light
To the darkness
Even if it is not
Understood
Or appreciated
It still shines
For them
Always

Nothing haunts me so

Leaving me quite as
puzzled as the
life I could
of lived.
If I had just
loved myself
and trusted
myself
from the very
beginning.

There are many
colors in my soul,
shining above
my treacherous sea.

Scared
Brave
Restless
Hopeful

and all of them
have a home,
deep inside of me.

If you've claimed to have
ever loved someone,
forgive them.
Like you've never
made a mistake.
Like you've never
had bad judgment.
You expected them
to forgive you, and they did.
Do you remember
how that forgiveness
helped you heal?
Do it for yourself.
To honor that forgiveness
you were once given.
Make it worth it
That doesn't mean
they have to be
a part of your life.
In fact they are out of it.
Out of your mind
Out of your heart
Forgive them. Let them go

-message to self

I like people with depth
With emotion
With soul
People that are not afraid
to be vulnerable.
People that speak their mind.
People who can make me
see the world differently.
In a way I've never seen it,
in a way I never realized
that I could see it.
People who can make me *feel*
Who want to bring me along
for the ride
in their perception.

In their world.

People who will
really care about me.
Where I can sense
that comfort.
Setting my soul at ease.

I like people like that.

You can't be strong
all the time.
Everything has to come
to an end.
Every flower dies
and withers away,
every petal disintegrates
from within.
When it's your time,
you too
will blossom again.

I am so labyrinthine
yet fascinating.
I am a complicated craft
not everyone
could really understand.
But I have
the biggest heart.
I care tremendously.
The ones that took
the time to see inside,
I changed their world.
I made them
think differently.
A new perspective
awaiting them.
A loyal friend to the end.
To listen to you,
to cry with, to laugh with.
Everything you could need,
I was there.
I was special and
they would never forget me.

I'm grateful to have lived
through darkness.
I don't think I'd have
the same appreciation
for this marvelously
sewn together heart,
if I had not once before
seen it violently
ripped apart,

like a child's teddy bear
torn into a million pieces.

Scattered everywhere.

She grew so weary
of running away
from storms.
Always running,
so she decided
to become one instead.
Unleashing her glorious fury
upon each and every head.
Now they all run from her,
spreading fear to
even the dead.

He was always one of
The quiet ones
She was commotion
On a blacktop
Their connection was so Astonishing
He didn't know
Where to start
She didn't know
When to stop

Patience is the
hardest one for me.
The waiting
The anticipation
The stress
I can't seem to
find it enjoyable.
My positivity is empty.
It's draining
There is still a
sense of gratitude
through the
process of discontent.
I've grown accustomed to it.
I'm not sure if I could
get through it with a light,
but I go through it,
just in the darkness.
If you think
I don't have patience, *I do.*
I just go through it differently.

Much more differently
than you.

Going through the hard times
Knowing I survived it all
Gives me a sense of pride
And strength
I cannot explain it
But I stand tall
The past
It still settles inside of me
Every single day
Sometimes the memories
Rush through my mind
Begging to come out and play
But I tuck them tight
And say goodnight
And go about my day

It's enlightening
and strange,
knowing you
can change.
Learning that
you have control.
Proving that
they were wrong.

You are worthy

You deserve
every gift,
every blessing,
every comfort,
and all of their love.
Every kiss,
every smile,
and every single hug.

My wonder is in her steps
My passion is in her cries
My beauty is in her face
My adventure is in her eyes
Myself undone
And made anew
She is where my
Happiness lies

Dear Daddy,

I never thought
it would happen.
I never thought
it could be.
I never thought
I would
love someone
as selflessly
as you love me.

One of the
greatest gifts
I'll ever receive
in this life
is having you for
a daughter.

Looking at her
I'm sure you'd think,

She's got everything

But what keeps
your attention
is that somehow
she doesn't
seem to care.

She still desires,
she always wants
more from this life.

Not everyone will
know your strength,
will listen to the stories
beneath your scars,
will understand
your trespasses.
But your not here
to make everyone
understand.
You're here to live your life.
So live it for you
and the ones
that love you.
The ones that do know,
have listened,
and do understand.

Because are they not
the only ones that
truly matter anyway?

Sometimes I
don't need advice.
I give myself
the very best advice.
My self awareness
has always been
my prized possession.
Sometimes all I want
is an ear to listen,
a shoulder to cry on,
and a heart to
not judge me.

How could anyone
take the emptiness.
Knowing that there is a wondrous
piece of yourself
out there in the world without you.

That you have never talked to
That you've never even known

It's an experience that I myself
could not imagine living without.

I would feel so alone

Remember being
with each other,
almost every single day.
Hanging out all the time
and then asking
one another to stay.
We were together so much
I never thought it would
just end this way.
We lost touch
with each other,
it all just stopped.
We drifted away,
it was all so abrupt.

Never looking for gold
she chased rainbows.
It was the magical feeling
of being alive
and enjoying life,
that was the real
treasure for her.
She never stopped,
she was always looking
for more.

I would not have
the option to
just simply die
without you,
my baby.
I would have to
do something
much torturously worse.
I would have to go on
trying my hardest
to stay strong.
Trying my best to
hang on
living without you.

When we were children
Innocently playing
Red rover on the
Playground
So blissfully unaware
We grasped on tightly
To each other
Without judgments
Without color
With no distinction
Challenging the world
To rip our grip
From one another

I wouldn't give back
one cry,
one colorful fit
of frustration,
one helpless glance.
Eyes filled with wonder
Not knowing what
you want,
or what to do.
I'd do it all over again
if it meant I'd go
through it with you.

I am darkness
I am light
I am happiness
I am regret
I am pride
I am shame
So simple
Yet complex
It is insane
Dripping
With such
Irony
No category
to place me in
Identifiable
Only as my name

There are times
in this world when
I get thrown into
powerful winds,
am showered with
heavy recurrent hail,
get hit with endless
lightening strikes.

I have built myself
up to withstand
the most dangerous
of storms.

So here I am
bring on the thunder
I dare you.

You think
a soul lies
only in a person.
A person that
speaks and
thinks like you,
but if you
can see past
the unfamiliar.
You'll learn
things
so beautiful
and true
you never knew.

I always open up,
I like to feel vulnerable,
I like to be understood.
I like when others
get to see inside.
Something about that
has always satisfied me.

To hear their response,
to know their thoughts,
to listen and
see their reaction.

To see how I am seen
Maybe even sometimes
honestly and openly

By you
and not just by me.

Would you believe me
if I told you
the truest
beauty resides
in the broken things.
To you
they are
just useless.
To me
they just need to be
remade.
The beauty is inside,
the memories
still remain.

They still have a story,
they are still special,
in there own
crazy useless way.

It's not about perfection.
It's not about always
getting everything right.
It's about the mistakes.
It's about the fights.
It's the sticking around
to figure things out.
It's having the conversations,
that's what love is all about.

She will never again
Tear herself apart
Never again torment
Over everything
Never again cry
Her heart out
She will be there
For herself
Day after day
Trying to heal
The wounds
That she has caused
All she can do
Is believe in herself
And pray
And pray
And pray

Her suffering
was not in vain.
It has allowed her
to unleash the
glue within,
that would put
her back together.

These dark circles
around my eyes
testify to the sleepless nights
I have spent with you.

Every cry you cried
Every time you
clutched my fingers
Every comforting coo

There is nothing I would
rather do,
then wear these
dark circles for you.

Because of you
I never seen
What giving up
Looks like
Because of you
I never felt
What true heartache
Feels like
Because of you
I never heard
What abandonment
Sounds like
I shall never know
What emptiness is
Because of you

At times it's hard
to remember
the lost person I once was.

The way she thought,
her perception of life,
her priorities,
her pain,
her innocence,

But other times
it's hard to forget.

Shatter my windows,
tear down the walls,
smash in my ceiling.
You can destroy it all.
My foundation will remain,
And I will always rebuild.
Never underestimate a woman
with perseverance
and free will.

He loved me
no matter
my past faults,
And understood
that there
was nothing
time hadn't
touched.

I am so much more
than any label you
can bestow upon me.
I am many things.
Not even I could
ever define myself
as but a single word.

I am a name
I am me
I am Ashleigh

ACKNOWLEDGMENTS

I want to thank a couple people for the extraordinary confidence and courage they gave me to release this book.

Ruby Dhal author of Memories Unwound @r.dhalwriter and Kayil York author of Roses and Thorns @rose_thorns1921 for all your motivating words when my anxiety and negative thoughts took over. The compassion and love within them meant the world to me.

Christina Strigas, my amazing editor, who encouraged me to have faith in myself and not be afraid to reveal who I truly am. That this honesty, my honesty, would help me heal from the shame I still felt from my past. This would not have happened without you.

Special thanks to my family, friends, and the love of my life Russell Sample, who had to listen to me talk about this book for over a year. I love you with all my heart.

Thank you to everyone that believed in me when at times I had trouble believing in myself.

ABOUT THE AUTHOR

My name is Ashleigh Marie Rayl. 25 years old. I am daughter to two extraordinarily strong parents that loved me and support-ed me always. I am a proud mother of two, a son and a daughter. I am a recovered addict and have seven years clean. I am currently living in Michigan, United States.

I write simply to express myself. I write of dreams, of all my whispering wonders, and of my past, present and future. I write to release things. I write to take myself back to certain places, and to help me go to certain places. I write so that I may never forget my triumphs and progress. I write to remember where I came from, who I was, and who I truly am.

Email: rayl103@comcast.net
Facebook: Ashleigh Rayl
Instagram: @ashrayl

Made in the USA
Lexington, KY
13 July 2018